DADS

DADS

Compiled by Rose O'Kelly

RONNIE
SELLERS
PRODUCTIONS
-Gift Books-

Dad: a son's first hero,
a daughter's first love.

Proverb

A father is neither an anchor to hold us back, nor a sail to take us there, but a guiding light whose love shows us the way.

George Webster Douglas

To her the name of father
was another name for love.

Fanny Fern

Your dad is the man who
does all the heavy shoveling
for your sandcastle, and
then tells you you've done
a wonderful job.

Rose O'Kelly

Only a father
doesn't begrudge
his son's talent.

Johann Wolfgang von Goethe

To an old father,
nothing is more sweet
Than a daughter.

Euripides

Like father, like son:
every good tree
maketh good fruits.

William Langland

Dad's great about showing us how to do stuff. Even if he doesn't really know what he's doing, he passes that knowledge on to us.

David Butler

Your father
is your shelter.

Anna Carr

The moving principle of his conduct through life was love for, and pride in, his father.

Author unknown

Any man can be a father,
but it takes someone
special to be a dad.

Proverb

'Tis a happy thing
To be the father unto
many sons.

William Shakespeare

Let him lie there, half waking, and rejoice
In the safe shelter of his resting-place,
In hearing of his…father's voice…

Caroline Wilder

Best father,
sweetest friend…

Lucy Robinson

My dad saw me make the most strange faces. I opened wide to be fed, I bawled, I scowled—and he put food in my mouth, and comforted me, and cheered me up, and still thought I was beautiful

Natasha Burns

A man's father
is his king.

Rabbi Eliezer

None of you can ever be proud enough of being the child of such a Father who has not his equal in this world—so great, so good, so faultless.

Queen Victoria

Sweet to the father is
his first-born's birth.

Lord Byron

Confident men have patient fathers.

Rose O'Kelly

A father is someone you look up to, no matter how tall you are.

Author unknown

I throw myself upon your breast,
    my father,
I cling to you so that you cannot
    unloose me…
Kiss me, my father,
Touch me with your lips, as I
    touch those I love,
Breathe to me, while I hold you
    close.

Walt Whitman

Such a father,
such a son.

William Camden

I associate the smell of new-cut grass with my father, and sunny days, and happiness.

Natasha Burns

The greatest gift
I ever had came from God...
I call him Dad.

Author unknown

There are three stages of man:
he believes in Santa Claus;
he does not believe in Santa Claus;
he *is* Santa Claus.

Bob Phillips

There are no days we
enjoy so much as those
shared with our father.

Iona Allford

He was her god,
the center of her
small world.

Margaret Mitchell

The sight that brings the
deepest pride to a father's
heart is his children
proud of themselves.

Rose O'Kelly

Directly after God
in heaven comes
a Papa.

Mozart

Captain!
dear father!

Walt Whitman

To bring up a child in the way he should go, travel that way yourself once in a while.

Josh Billings

How sweet 'tis to sit 'neath
a fond father's smile…

John Howard Payne

A wise son heareth his
father's instructions.

The Bible

Do dads talk about calories, or cavities, or spoiling your appetite? No! Dads grab themselves a spoon and dig right in with you.

Anna Carr

My father was an
amazing man.
The older I got,
the smarter he got.

Mark Twain

O dearest, dearest boy! my heart
For better lore would seldom yearn,
Could I but teach the hundredth part
Of what from thee I learn.

William Wordsworth

Daughters can never take
too much care of their father.

Plautus

He that honoreth his father shall have a long life.

The Bible

My dad always knew how to make a fire on a cold day and where to get the best ice cream on a hot one. Whenever the world got too much for me, he was right on the job.

Natasha Burns

My father's busy
...but he always
has time for me.

Judy Blume

No music is so
pleasant to my ears
as that word—father.

Lydia Maria Child

Small boys become big men through the influence of big men who care about small boys.

Anonymous

Sometimes the person I want to see more than anyone in the world is my dad.

Sharon Dennis Wyeth

My Dad is brilliant...
It's great having a dad
like mine. It's brilliant.

Nick Butterworth

91

These moments alone with my father were the most peaceful and contented moments of my childhood.

Natasha Burns

They are splendid people
and their absolute love of
their children places them
above the highest praise.

Anton Chekhov

A wise son maketh a glad father.

The Bible

He who can be a good son
will be a good father.

Chinese proverb

Blessed indeed is
the man who hears
many gentle voices
calling him father!

Lydia Maria Child

My dad was John Wayne, Superman, King Arthur; he was my hero.

Anna Carr

Be kind to thy father, for when
    thou wert young,
Who loved thee so fondly as he?
He caught the first accents that
    fell from thy tongue,
And joined thee in innocent glee.

Margaret Courtney

We like to hop
on Pop.

Dr. Seuss

By the light of my father's smile

Alice Walker

Picture Credits

All images © Getty Images, unless otherwise stated.

Text Credits

Published by Ronnie Sellers Productions, Inc.

P.O. Box 818, Portland, Maine 04104
For ordering information:
Telephone: (800) MAKE-FUN (625-3386)
Fax: (207) 772-6814
Visit our Web site: www.makefun.com
E-mail: rsp@rsvp.com

First published by MQ Publications Limited
12 The Ivories. 6-8 Northampton Street, London, United Kingdom

Copyright © MQ Publications Limited 2003

Text compilation: Rose O'Kelly
Design: Philippa Jarvis

ISBN: 1-56906-515-2

Printed and bound in China.